DIGITAL AND INFORMATION LITERACY ™

GETTING THE MOST OUT OF MOOC:
MASSIVE OPEN ONLINE COURSES

RITA LORRAINE HUBBARD

rosen publishing's
**rosen
central**

New York

To my sons Thomas D. Hubbard and Marcus D. Hubbard,
who are digital giants in their own right

Published in 2015 by The Rosen Publishing Group, Inc.
29 East 21st Street, New York, NY 10010

Library of Congress Cataloging-in-Publication Data

Hubbard, Rita L., author.
Getting the most out of MOOC: massive open online courses/Rita Lorraine Hubbard.—First edition.
    pages cm.—(Digital and information literacy)
Includes bibliographical references and index.
ISBN 978-1-4777-7950-7 (library bound)—ISBN 978-1-4777-7951-4 (pbk.)—ISBN 978-1-4777-7952-1 (6-pack)
1. MOOCs (Web-based instruction)—Juvenile literature. 2. Distance education—Juvenile literature. 3. Educational technology—Juvenile literature. I. Title. II. Title: Massive open online courses. III. Series: Digital and information literacy.
LB1044.87.H83 2015
371.35'8—dc23

2014011786

Manufactured in Malaysia

CONTENTS

INTRODUCTION

If you are familiar with the term "MOOC," you probably know that it stands for "massive open online courses." You probably also know that these courses are delivered via Internet to any person wishing to enroll and that there is no limit to class size and usually no fee involved. But if you are thinking of signing up for a MOOC, you need to know much more than this.

You should know that MOOCs are about accessing information that, because of the class location or fee involved, may not have been available to you otherwise. They're about a unique opportunity to customize your own education, and they are about connecting locally, nationally, or globally with other people who have interests similar to your own. MOOCs don't discriminate according to age, location, financial status, or test scores; they are for everyone.

Because the majority of MOOCs are designed and taught by college professors, it is logical that most will resemble the fast-paced, independent classroom style of typical brick-and-mortar college courses. This is a plus for teens who may be considering college at some point in the future because they get to experience the subject matter firsthand (albeit virtually) and decide whether they even like it. Some teens even use MOOCs from

You can use your favorite search engine to browse a list of MOOCs that you will be able to access free of charge, from the comfort of your home.

specific colleges as a sort of "virtual tour" of what the college and its courses will be like.

But MOOCs are also for students who are already enrolled in college. College students often use MOOCs to brush up on certain skills (e.g., math, technical writing, or a foreign language) or to supplement their curriculum. Teachers and college professors use MOOCs, too, for a variety of reasons, including learning how to create their own MOOCs to teach.

Although MOOCs are designed to be educational, they are not limited to those in the education field or those who are thinking of entering an institution of higher learning. Everyday people use them to spice up their lives, learn about other cultures, brush up on their personal skills, sharpen their English, pursue a subject or concept they never got around to when they were younger, or simply continue along their dedicated path to becoming a lifelong learner.

To survive in this virtual world of independent learning, you will need to know how to perform MOOC searches, how to differentiate a quality MOOC from a substandard one, who produces the most reputable MOOCs, which MOOCs offer continuing education or college credit, and how to recognize which MOOCs are just for fun. In other words, you need to become "MOOC-literate."

Chapter 1

MOOCs vs. Traditional Higher-Education Courses

Becoming MOOC-literate means being able to perform an in-depth exploration of the MOOC model and all it has to offer. But first it may be best to explain the traditional college model.

The College Course Model

When students with a high school diploma or GED decide to go to college, they complete an application for entry. They visit the college campus for orientation, and once they are approved for admission, they declare a major and speak with an advisor. They enroll in required and elective classes in their chosen field. Before they can attend those classes, however, they must pay the fees, often with the help of student loans or financial aid, and purchase the required textbooks from which the courses will be taught. These steps may not necessarily occur in this order, but in general, these are the things that must occur before students can begin their college classes.

Although there may be variations, most of the courses are delivered in small settings with a professor, a teacher's assistant (sometimes), and a limited number of students. The students receive a course syllabus, listen to classroom lectures by the professor, and participate in discussions and question-and-answer sessions with the professor or the teacher's assistant.

Students may or may not be required to complete lab work, fieldwork, or a practicum period. They may or may not take a midterm exam, but they usually must earn a passing score on a final exam to move to the next level of courses in the field.

Tests, pop quizzes, and exams are usually graded by the professor or teacher's assistant, and the grade(s) earned dictate whether the student can move forward to the next level in the program. If a student earns a failing grade, he or she would need to decide if it is best to try again or withdraw from that particular course of study and declare a different major. The student can use this time of reflection to drop by the professor's office during his or her prescheduled office hours to discuss remedies and options.

A typical college bookstore is chaotic before the first day of school, when students scramble to locate and purchase the books they will need for their classes.

If the student decides to declare a different major, he or she would need to get the advisor's approval before doing so, and the student can only enroll in the new courses if the classes are not full.

The MOOC Course Model

The MOOC course model is completely different, mainly because there has never been a real MOOC model. While traditional college students usually pay dearly for their courses, most MOOCs are offered free of charge, meaning there is typically no need to pay cash, apply for financial aid, or borrow money from friends and family to take the courses.

Since the classes are offered via the Internet and involve other technologies like Skype, webinar, video, podcast and/or Google Chat, there are no

MOOCs are "classes without borders" that can be accessed by anyone anywhere in the world as long as the learner has a strong Internet connection and a high interest in learning.

Most MOOC students already hold a college degree, but their lifelong love of learning leads them to continued educational opportunities, especially when the classes are both free and convenient.

geographical limitations. Students can enroll from anywhere on the globe as long as the class is being offered in a language that they understand.

Because the courses are virtual, there are no size limits. For example, one free course listed on MOOC provider Udemy's website has more than thirty-two thousand students enrolled. Another course called Circuits and Electronics was launched by MIT professor Anant Agarwal in the hopes of enticing at least 1,500 students to enroll. The final enrollment was 150,000.

Because MOOCs have no enrollment limits, students do not interact with each other as they would in a regular college course. With class sizes numbering in the tens to hundreds of thousands, students must be self-reliant.

College courses usually lead to a degree, but MOOCs are usually stand-alone courses that do not. Also, most MOOC students are not like typical incoming college freshmen who have never experienced higher-learning classes. The majority of MOOC students already hold a bachelor's degree or higher, and the rest are either students who are

File   Edit   View   Favorites   Tools   Help

WHERE TO FIND THE MOOCS

Where to Find the MOOCs

MOOC providers are popping up everywhere. Four of the better-known providers are Coursera, edX, Udacity, and Udemy. Coursera's seventy-three universities (including Harvard, MIT, and Stanford) offer more than five hundred courses in such subjects as computer science, history, health care policy, and English literature to more than twenty-two million enrollees. EdX is a nonprofit that partners with twenty-eight institutions (including MIT, Harvard, UC Berkeley, and Dartmouth) to offer sixty courses (including biology, business, chemistry, computer science, and law) to over one million registered students. Udacity partners with Georgia Tech and San Jose State to service more than 750,000 students enrolled in thirty courses that focus on "cutting edge technology education." Udemy, which is a bit of a newcomer, has published more than twelve thousand courses for its over two hundred million students and adds over eight hundred new courses every month.

currently enrolled in a college and are supplementing their education in their own way, students who yearn to take classes from a certain professor but have no other way to accomplish this except to enroll in the professor's MOOC, or professionals or continuing-education students who are looking for personal enrichment.

In traditional college courses, class attendance is mandatory and excessive absences may lead to forced withdrawal from a class, or worse, a failing grade. Not so with MOOCs. Although many of the more recent MOOCs follow a defined schedule like traditional classes (synchronous rotation), the lecture models are recorded so that students can study at their own convenience within a certain window of time. These recorded lecture models are usually twelve to fifteen minutes in length, which is much shorter than the typical forty-five-minute live classroom lecture. This shortened presentation is usually more easily digested by students who have little or no interaction with college professors.

Since many MOOC enrollees are not working toward a college degree, the tests, quizzes, and exams (if any) associated with classes don't have the same weight as those in a traditional college course. In fact, *Massive Open Online Courses (MOOCs) Primer for University and College Board Members* explains that because the courses are free, "no certified value for their learning assessments has yet been established." Also, because there may be tens of thousands of students enrolled in the same class, the ability to give each student feedback about his or her performance is highly limited, and some course tests, quizzes, and exams must be peer-graded for convenience.

Stanford University computer science professors Andrew Ng and Daphne Koller launched Coursera in 2012. It now attracts people from every walk of life around the world.

Another difference between the MOOC "non-model" and the traditional college model relates to demographics. In an article in the *Atlantic*, Coursera cofounder Daphne Koller says that most MOOC courses "attract a largely international student body; 60–67 percent of the students come from the international community, but those numbers vary depending on the topic and the course."

Perhaps the biggest difference between MOOCs and traditional college courses is in the final number of students completing the courses. According to various sources, MOOC completion ranges from 5 to 10 percent. So if a course enrolls 150,000 students, only 7,500 to 15,000 students will actually complete the course.

MYTHS & FACTS

MYTH All MOOCs are free.

FACT While most MOOCs are free, others charge a fee, depending on the subject. Also, many colleges are beginning to look at ways to defray the exorbitant cost of making MOOCs by charging a small fee.

MYTH MOOCs are only for college students.

FACT Although most MOOCs are accessed by students who are in college or who already hold a degree, many are accessed by professionals seeking to enhance their skills, high school students preparing to go to college, or continuing-education students wanting to enhance their personal lives.

MYTH The low rate of class completion means MOOCs are a failure.

FACT A 5- to10-percent completion rate would certainly be disastrous for the typical college class that enrolls thirty or more students because only one to three students would complete the class. But a MOOC with unlimited enrollment may have ten thousand students enrolled, and the same 5- to 10-percent completion rate would mean that five hundred to one thousand students completed the class. Successfully educating and graduating this many students from one class is no small feat.

Chapter 2

MOOCs vs. Other Paid Online Courses

Some of the most well-known MOOC producers include Coursera, edX, Udacity, and Udemy. Between them, they offer some 1,300 courses to millions of students worldwide. Their courses originate from prestigious universities like Stanford, Dartmouth, Harvard, MIT, and Berkeley, and the subjects include computer science, history, health care, literature,

Professors from prestigious universities, like MIT's Anant Agarwal, president of edX (*far right*), have partnered with online education platforms to offer classes in computer science, health care, biology, finance, and more.

business, biology, economics, and finance. However, there are other MOOC producers out there, as well as other types of online courses.

Private Online Universities

The University of Phoenix and Strayer University are two of several private for-profit institutions that offer online classes. Their class sizes are generally capped, in contrast to the unlimited enrollment of the typical MOOC. They also thrive on student-based tuition. An October 2013 report by BeyondProxy.com reveals that the University of Phoenix's tuition was among the highest of the for-profit universities.

The University of Phoenix and the most popular MOOC producers are similar in that the number of graduates is low in comparison to the number

Strayer University's strategy is to marry classroom and online learning. This combination reaches more students and helps them decide for themselves which method of learning is best for them.

of students enrolled in the courses. The only difference is that MOOC dropouts typically walk away with no debt and no failing grades on their records, while Phoenix dropouts (or those who simply don't graduate) walk away with massive debt and poor grades that must be repaired on their transcripts.

Strayer University's course model also differs from the typical MOOC model. Strayer uses a carefully blended combination of classroom and online learning in an effort to reach more students and allow them to decide which learning mode is best for them.

File   Edit   View   Favorites   Tools   Help

CUSTOMIZING YOUR EDUCATION

Customizing Your Education

Some scholars argue that people don't learn anything they don't want to learn. Thanks to thousands of free MOOCs being offered, it is now possible to learn exactly what you want to learn at your own pace. The more than 1,300 courses in computer science, history, health care, literature, business, biology, and more being offered by prestigious universities like Stanford, Dartmouth, Harvard, MIT, and Berkeley are like ripe fruit ready to be picked.

Most are free and have no age or enrollment limitations, and although you probably won't receive a degree, you may be eligible for some sort of certificate. All you need is to decide what you want to learn and then use the MOOC links to find the courses. For example, to learn about business, you could conduct an Internet search for a local or well-known university that offers business degrees. Scan and copy the list of classes included in the business degree and then begin searching anyplace you like. In this case, perhaps a course called Entrepreneurism is included in the list. You can begin your business education by searching the Internet and browsing the many MOOCs to find a course in entrepreneurism.

Although Strayer believes that having access to online classes gives students more flexibility, it does not believe that an online education will fully replace classroom-based learning. It also frowns upon the concept of mass enrollment in online classes because it limits peer-to-peer and faculty interaction.

Students can pursue almost all the degrees that Strayer offers via distance education. However, unlike the typical MOOC structure, Strayer prefers not to leave its online students to their own devices. Its administrators say they have "spent thousands of hours perfecting the way [they] teach and support [their] students online." To finance these classes or degree programs, students must have access to cash, private loans, and/or federal student aid programs.

Pros and Cons of MOOCs vs. Private Online Universities

When you compare MOOCs to for-profit online educational institutions, there are several pros and cons. One MOOC pro is that there is no cost of attendance, which has fueled a drop in registrations at for-profit online educational institutions like Strayer and Phoenix. Students have begun to question what they feel are exorbitant tuition fees to enroll in those universities, especially when they can't guarantee that they will land a job after graduation. MOOCs don't have this problem because most of them cost nothing, can be completed at the student's whim, and pose no penalty if the student withdraws.

Another pro is that edX, Coursera, Udacity, and Udemy all offer MOOCs from respected universities and the high-profile professors who teach there. When students enroll in these courses, they gain a bit of prestige because they can show (with a certificate of completion or achievement) that they have received instruction from an admired university or professor.

One con is that MOOCs lag behind traditional online university courses in terms of quality. Although some MOOCs offer coveted quality

This professor is answering a student's question during a crucial exam, but this type of one-on-one teacher-student interaction is often impossible in a MOOC, in which thousands of students might be enrolled.

courses taught by high-profile professors, many lack any sort of structure. Also, due to sheer size alone, they are sorely lacking in opportunities for student-teacher and peer-to-peer interaction. Instructor grading is nearly impossible, peer-to-peer grading is almost always implemented, and cheating is an ugly reality.

Another con is that MOOCs are "self-guided" classes that don't offer credits and don't typically lead to a degree of any kind. Because of this structure (or lack thereof), students who enroll may be ill-equipped for true college courses because the two models are so different. For these reasons,

MOOCs are often abandoned by students who haven't invested anything to enroll, are not expecting to gain anything upon completion, and know they will not be punished if they decide to withdraw.

Fortunately, the pros seem to hold their own against the cons. According to a 2013 study conducted by Duke University researchers Yvonne Belanger and Jessica Thornton, "Student motivation [to enroll in MOOCs] typically fell into one of four categories:

- To support lifelong learning or gain an understanding of the subject matter with no particular expectations for completion or achievement
- For fun, entertainment, social experience, and intellectual stimulation
- Convenience, often in conjunction with barriers to traditional education options
- To experience or explore online education."

Chapter 3

Ten Tips for Becoming MOOC-Literate

OOCs are everywhere. Big, distinguished universities are making tens of thousands of them available for anyone interested in learning. Smaller, private online platforms also offer them on almost any topic you can think of. Businesses offer them for continuing education for their employees, and even elementary schools create them for teachers, administrators, and students.

It's easy to find MOOCs. Just type the word "MOOC" into your favorite search engine, and you will instantly be a click away from millions of links to everything MOOC. It's probably just as easy to enroll in a MOOC as it is to find one, but given the shockingly high rate of MOOC abandonment, how can you know if you're choosing the right MOOC or if you even have what it takes to complete it?

You need to become MOOC-literate. In other words, you need to understand how MOOCs operate in order to be successful. Following are tips to help you on your way.

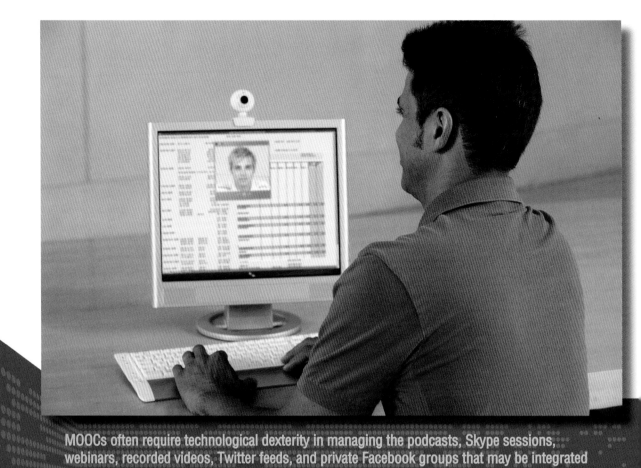

MOOCs often require technological dexterity in managing the podcasts, Skype sessions, webinars, recorded videos, Twitter feeds, and private Facebook groups that may be integrated into your class.

Step 1: Technology Doesn't Just Mean the Internet

To get the most out of MOOCs, you'll need to access and understand other technologies besides the Internet. For example, your MOOC will probably have prerecorded videos, but it might also include live lectures via Skype or Google+ Circles. You might be expected to utilize podcasts and webinars. You might need to understand how to create and share PDFs and white papers. You will probably be expected to join social networking sites like Facebook or Twitter, where you will join private groups for live chats and activities. Your class might create its own Meetup page or interact with the instructor through message boards. Whatever the means of access and interaction, you will need to be fluent in order to participate.

Step 2: You Must Be Willing to Invest the Time

Enrolling in and completing a MOOC can take time. Like traditional classes, MOOCs have various durations. Some last for one day, while others can last from one week to several months. The information in the MOOC may be broken down into several large chunks, including multiple videos or webinars that run from a few minutes to an hour or so in length three times per week. So if you enroll, you must be willing to commit to the duration. In addition, some MOOCs include quizzes, tests, and homework that may take you some time to complete. In other words, MOOCs are actual classes, even though they are served in virtual form and don't typically lead to a degree of any sort. Before you enroll, be sure to investigate thoroughly so that you will know what is required.

Even if your free MOOC is penalty-free in terms of grading, fees, and class completion, organize your schedule and commit to the time and effort it will take to complete it.

23

Step 3: MOOCs Don't Always Have Prerequisites

"Prerequisite" means something that is required before you can do something else. Prerequisite classes can be like a barrier that blocks the learner from the classes that he or she is really interested in. The good news is that most MOOCs are stand-alone classes, meaning they are independent and not meant to lead into any other class. The bad news is that this can be a problem when it comes to comprehension because stand-alone classes are

The Advantage of Free Courses

Aside from the obvious benefit of not having to pay for them, MOOCs are extremely beneficial for students at or below the poverty level or students from third world countries who have limited or no access to books or higher education. According to George Siemens, Canada's "MOOC Pioneer" and the principal investigator of the Bill & Melinda Gates Foundation's MOOC Research Initiative, "Projects like this can impact lives around the world… There are now [almost] 10 million students internationally who are able to access free, open, online education. That's the equivalent of opening 40, 50 or more universities." According to Siemens, these people "are getting educational opportunities that result in actual employment." Alternately, pumping education into these third world countries may well open the door to what Siemens calls the opportunity to "export their knowledge," which means that once they begin reciprocating the knowledge, "we [the United States] will have a better understanding of the issues that might exist in Africa, Latin America, China, or India."

designed with the assumption that you are already familiar with all the concepts, vocabulary, formulas, calculations, etc., that are included in the class. If you're not, you will need to bring yourself up to speed quickly. Otherwise, you will have a hard time comprehending the material and holding your own in class.

Step 4: MOOCs May Not Challenge You Enough

Like many brick-and-mortar classes, some MOOCs are simply not challenging enough. Some are hastily written and include drab videos and one-dimensional materials and exams that are thrown together to document that some type of assessment is being offered. The fact is, MOOCs can be very expensive to produce, costing tens of thousands of dollars on the front end and earning nothing on the back end. For this reason, many are low in quality and offer no real interaction from the teacher, the students, or even the exams. Perri Bronson, in an article on Tivix.com, explains that "most MOOCs are consumed during the hours of 9 PM and 2 AM after regular work/school hours, so these courses face the challenge of being stimulating enough to keep people interested (and awake)."

Step 5: MOOCs May Vary in Quality

Unfortunately, not all MOOCs are professionally produced. Some are simply an attempt to bring brick-and-mortar classes to the Internet, and as such, are a complete failure. Some consist of lengthy videos in which professors simply read from PowerPoint slides. Other MOOCs have even longer videos that are rarely taken down and replaced by new material. They may even include numerous reading assignments and "canned" questions that attempt to assess what has been learned. These poorly constructed MOOCs can dishearten even the most avid learner, so the key is to recognize a bad MOOC and parachute away before you waste too much time.

Step 6: You Have to Love Lectures

Although the MOOC structure is improving every day, many MOOCs rely heavily on video lectures that may last anywhere from several minutes to well in excess of an hour—and there may be three to four of these lessons per week. If you get bored listening to long, drawn-out lecturing in a "live" classroom, you'll almost certainly be bored to tears in a lengthy MOOC lecture. But since lecturing plays a big part in the classroom, it's something you should prepare yourself for.

If you have a hard time staying focused during a live lecture like this one, you may find the long, prerecorded lectures in the typical MOOC to be quite a challenge.

Step 7: Your Teacher and Classmates May Be Invisible

Although a MOOC is a sort of classroom, it is not made of brick and mortar. There is a certain level of aloneness that comes with this type of educational platform. Even if your best friend enrolls in the same MOOC at the same time, you still may not get to interact with him or her. The fact is you may be all alone in your MOOC, especially if there are thousands or tens of thousands of students enrolled at the same time. Large MOOCs can give you the sensation of being lost in the crowd. Even if the MOOC offers corresponding student groups and forums, these may simply be too big, too diverse, or too complex to keep up with. Even worse, the more students enrolled in the class, the more likely it is that your professor won't have time to interact with you or the other students. Instead, the professor may leave feedback, grading, and question-and-answer sessions to your invisible peers. This can be disheartening and a little bit lonely, but recognizing it before you make the leap will prepare you.

Step 8: Just Because the MOOC Is Free Doesn't Mean the Books Are

Because most MOOCs are free, many virtual students are lured into signing up to take advantage of their rich content. But many drop the classes just as quickly when they discover that the course calls for textbooks (many written by the instructor) that must be purchased in conjunction with the course. According to Jennifer Howard, "Publishers have begun to investigate whether so-called MOOCs...can help them reach new readers and sell more books." Even if the instructor does not require students to purchase textbooks, there may be a small handout fee or an associated fee for a required reading list. Some instructors even offer book rentals to defray costs, but a rental still involves a fee.

Step 9: You Probably Won't Get Credit for Your MOOC

The good news is that MOOCs are open to everyone and you can study practically anything you want. The not-so-good news is that once you complete your MOOC, you may not be able to use it to further your education or career. The sad fact is, offering full accreditation for a cost-free MOOC actually works against MOOC providers who spend tens of thousands of dollars producing quality MOOCs for virtual students. If they offered free accreditation, students wouldn't need to bother enrolling in their costly brick-and-mortar classes on the same subjects.

According to Open Culture's MOOC FAQs, providers do offer an alternative: "Many…will give students a Certificate of Completion, Statement of Accomplishment or some other equivalent if students successfully complete a course [but]…you generally cannot take the certificate to your university and get actual credit." However, according to EdtechMagazine.com, Tricia Bishop of the University of Maryland says students can get credit for certain courses that match certain universities' offerings "as long as they can prove they know the material, and as long as they take a paid version of the course for $150 or less, which includes proctored exams." Bishop also says the students could opt to go through a rigorous "prior learning assessment" that measures competency. Whichever route students choose, Bishop says they shouldn't "think we're giving away credit."

Step 10: You May Have to Pay for Your Completion Certificate

If you successfully complete your MOOC(s), you should be proud of yourself. The current MOOC dropout rate is phenomenal, simply because there are no prerequisites to enroll and no penalties to withdraw, and most people only enroll out of curiosity. Most of these free MOOCs offer certificates of completion, but some may supply a variation (e.g., certificate of achievement) for a nominal fee.

As the quality and scope of MOOCs evolve, so does the question of how to make them pay for themselves. MOOCs are expensive to produce, so it would not be beneficial to give away college credits along with the free information. For these reasons, various schools and academies are exploring ways to make MOOCs worthwhile for the producers.

According to a MOOC Directory article, "if you want to showcase your MOOC courses and achievements to employers, schools, and others, a new optional type of paid 'Verified Certificate' credential is available that verifies that it was you who enrolled in and completed the MOOC." Coursera offers a Signature Track certificate program in which, for a nominal fee ($30–$100), your identity is verified and you get proof of course completion and verification of the grade you earned for your performance. Other agencies, institutions, and universities are also coming on board and offering verified certificates for a fee, mainly because MOOCs simply won't be free forever. Sooner or later, they will cost you.

TEN GREAT QUESTIONS
TO ASK PROSPECTIVE EMPLOYERS

1 How do you feel about MOOCs?

2 Would you consider a MOOC as a way to advance in your company?

3 Do you reimburse MOOC fees for successful completion of the course and accompanying certificate?

4 Do you offer incentives or credits for MOOCs?

5 Will you accept MOOCs as a type of in-service program?

6 Are there any company-created MOOCs for employees?

7 Can you suggest MOOCs that you think might benefit me as your employee?

8 Can you offer me corporate credit for the MOOCs I choose?

9 Can a MOOC qualify me for a raise?

10 Do you know of others enrolled in MOOCs whom I can partner with?

Chapter 4

Experiencing a MOOC Course

o enroll in a MOOC, you must first decide which platform you will use: Coursera, edX, Udacity, or Udemy. There are other platforms out there, but you can begin with one of these.

Typically, you will register via Facebook or your e-mail address. Once this is done, you will receive an e-mail asking you to verify that you've actually enrolled. Now you are ready to choose your MOOC. Choosing can be quite complicated because some MOOC providers offer thousands of courses at any given time, and some of these are duplicate topics taught by different instructors. In this case, the easiest way to choose would be to type what you want to learn into the search bar to see if a class is being offered. Unfortunately, some MOOC platforms don't have an advanced search bar. This means you must scroll page by page to see what types of MOOCs are being offered—a disheartening activity that might actually overwhelm you and make you change your mind about enrolling.

The Virtual Classroom

Justin Pope became one of 39,600 to sign up for a certain MOOC. The class was free, so there was no payment, and the only tools necessary were the recommended text and the homework assignments that he would need to submit.

According to Pope, the experience was simple enough because "an online 'dashboard' gives you access to videos, quizzes, and other resources. You quickly fall into a routine: a video lecture segment by one of the professors [that] typically lasts five to fifteen minutes, followed by exercises to make sure you got the key points, plus a longer homework assignment after each week."

This scenario sounds easy enough, but Pope says the class was difficult because it offered no credits upon completion, required "a minimum of 2–3

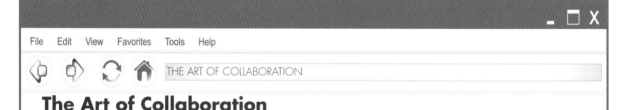

File   Edit   View   Favorites   Tools   Help

THE ART OF COLLABORATION

The Art of Collaboration

Collaboration is "the action of working with someone to produce or create something." Even though it will seem that you are alone in your MOOC, this doesn't have to be the case. First, don't be a "forever lurker," meaning don't remain silent throughout the entire course. Reach out and say hello, post positive comments about other students' progress, and speak up about concepts or issues in the course that interest you. Next, become a part of a group. Most MOOCs have student forums, but even if your MOOC doesn't, try to start a Facebook or Twitter group. If this doesn't work, send out an ad-like comment asking for a MOOC buddy to study with. Once you form a group or find a buddy, don't end the collaboration just because the MOOC ends. Keep networking.

hours per week of lectures, plus quizzes, homework and reading…and you have to keep up for 12 to 15 weeks." There was no face time with professors, and unlike high schools and colleges where a counselor's or advisor's door is always open, there was no office to drop by to discuss problems or concerns. Pope was on his own, except during those "weekly office hours run via chat by TAs [teaching assistants], but they picked eight submitters to Skype with and then posted the transcript."

Because MOOCs do not typically offer a self-paced model of learning, all students begin the course at the same time and proceed on the same schedule. This means that if a student has trouble with any of the concepts, he or she can't stop the course and ask the professor to explain. Also, if a student needs to be absent from the class, he or she can't turn in work ahead of schedule or make up work that was not completed.

Pope describes the process of answering students' questions as "a kind of lottery system [where] the professors picked a few questions and

Enrolling in a MOOC is as simple as deciding what you want to study and which provider you want to use. Here, instructors from the University of Pennsylvania record a live MOOC session on the subject of mythology.

posted replies." As for class participation, he describes what he considered a "big" thing: "I never made an argument. I was graded almost entirely on multiple-choice questions (sometimes we were asked for a number)." In other words, he never verbally explained anything, he never put forth a verbal or written argument or opinion, and he never expressed himself in written form other than to indicate the correct answer to a multiple-choice question.

Though he struggled to stay motivated, Pope did complete the class to become one of only 4,600 to finish in this class that originally had 39,600 enrollees.

Chapter 5

A MOOC for Everyone

MOOCs are spreading fast, and new opportunities are presenting themselves every day. For example, MOOCs were originally designed for college students, teachers, and continuing-education students. Now young adults, seniors, foreign students, third world students, high school students, and even elementary and middle grade students are accessing MOOCs.

MOOCs for K–12 Students

According to K12MOOC.org, "There is a global teacher shortage, and MOOCs can help fill the void." Research shows that the United States will need nearly 250,000 new math and science teachers by 2024, so there is discussion about allowing K–12 master teachers to begin sharing their classes via MOOC instruction. These same MOOCs might be utilized by beginning teachers as a vital professional resource and as supplemental materials to instruct their students. Alternately, they may be accessed by educational communities across the globe to "ensure universal access to a primary education by 2015."

Teachers can use MOOCs for everything from honing their own teaching skills to learning how to create their own MOOCs. They can also provide exciting supplemental materials for their tech-savvy students.

Very young children will need training and supervision to access the MOOCs and glean information from them. However, the opportunity to customize their education will be quite amazing. With MOOCs, accelerated students can learn new skills without disrupting the classroom, and remedial students can get the help they need in the privacy of their own homes (or in the school computer lab). MOOCs can even be designed to help elementary students transition to middle school and middle school students to transition to high school.

MOOCs for High School

MOOCs are becoming more and more popular in high schools. Some students use MOOCs instead of tutors, and others use MOOCs to give them an idea of the intensity level and factual requirements of a course or set of courses they will take when they enter college. According to RedefinED.com, "High schools can use MOOCs to more easily and cost-effectively supplement their

File   Edit   View   Favorites   Tools   Help

MOST POPULAR MOOCS

Most Popular MOOCs

In 2011, when MOOCs first started to emerge, the most popular courses centered around computer science. But later, humanities classes, which can encompass a variety of subjects, gained traction and surpassed computer science in number of offerings. MOOCs about databases, finance, English composition, programming, and math are also quite popular. Language MOOCs are popular, too, with Spanish and French topping the list.

curriculum . . . [They can] potentially help students customize their learning and provide an opportunity to increase digital learning skills. They can also be another tool to help determine if high school students are ready for college-level courses and, if they're not, to get them help before they spend time and money on remediation in college." In other words, MOOCs can be used as remedial instruction as high school students prepare for college.

MOOCs Instead of College

Search engines are brimming with articles about getting a college education without going to college. Platforms like Udemy, iTunes, Stanford Free Courses, UC Berkeley's Free Courses, and UCLA Free Courses (to name just a few) offer courses for educational enrichment and even accept certificates of completion for college credits.

The clever student can earn a degree in almost any way imaginable, including a "one-year MOOC BA." Jeff Schmitt offers a step-by-step approach to earning a college degree via MOOC education. He identifies what he calls "the complete core MBA curriculum" that is necessary for the degree and offers website links to each course for easy enrollment.

Even if students don't attempt to earn a full degree via MOOC education, it is still easier than ever for them to transfer their MOOC education into a more formal program of study. As mentioned earlier, many colleges are now offering "paid verified certificates," meaning that once you successfully complete your MOOC, you can pay a predetermined fee to verify your performance. This verification is accepted at certain colleges that then transfer the verification into college credits.

MOOCs for a Great Job

At this point in time, most MOOCs can't land you a degree, but they can definitely enhance your chances for getting a great job. You can acquire

Employers like degrees, but they also like employees with outstanding skills. The right MOOC can enhance your job skills and inspire an employer to bring you on board even if you don't have a degree.

skills that are helpful in the real world and desirable to employers. By accessing MOOCs, you can learn finance, computer literacy, artificial intelligence, business, and statistics—some of the most popular categories—as well as those that help a résumé stand out. Often, if you can demonstrate these skills, your employer might not care whether you have an actual diploma or not.

Because MOOCs utilize professors of high stature who come from Stanford, Harvard, MIT, and the like, employers should feel comfortable with the quality of the classes. Also, more and more MOOCs are offering verified certificates of completion and certificates of achievement, so employers are able to see what type of instruction you have received and how well you performed. According to a CampusExplorer.com article, "A certificate from a MOOC with the name of a respected college or university attached shows you have new, usable job skills, you are self-reliant, and you're always looking for ways to improve yourself. This gives you the competitive edge you need to snag your dream career."

And so, MOOCs are here to stay. They are free, they are evolving every day, and many are being taught by America's brightest professors. All a student of any age has to do is decide what interests him or her, conduct a bit of research, and jump right in.

GLOSSARY

certificate An official document attesting a certain fact, such as the successful completion of a MOOC.

con An argument or point against an issue.

credit A unit that gives weight to the value, level, or time requirements of an academic course taken at a school or other educational institution; also called a credit hour.

demographics Data, usually statistical, relating to the qualities of a particular population and the people living within it.

for-profit For financial gain, usually regarding the difference between the amount spent to buy, operate, or produce something and the amount actually earned.

nonprofit An organization that is not conducted primarily to make a profit.

podcast A multimedia digital file, usually of a program or other broadcast, made available on the Internet that can be downloaded to a media player, computer, cell phone, etc.

practicum A course of study for students, especially those aspiring to careers in fields involving teaching or clinical trials, that entails working in the area of study and using the knowledge and skills that have been learned in a school.

reciprocate To respond to something by making a similar gesture or action.

syllabus The outline of the subjects in a course of study.

synchronous Existing or occurring at the same time.

third world Of or relating to the developing countries of Asia, Africa, and Latin America; also, the countries themselves.

virtual Describes something created by computer science, simulated, or carried on by means of a computer or a computer network.

webinar A seminar conducted over the Internet.

white paper An authoritative report giving information or proposals on an issue.

FOR MORE INFORMATION

American Library Association (ALA)
50 E. Huron Street
Chicago, IL 60611
(800) 545-2433
Website: http://www.ala.org
The oldest and largest library association in the world, the ALA promotes
continuous, lifelong learning for all people through library and information services. It also offers support for librarians and others
interested in learning more about MOOCs, as well as webinars and
articles on the subject.

Inside Higher Ed
1015 18th Street NW, Suite 1100
Washington, DC 20036
(202) 659-9208
Website: http://www.insidehighered.com
Inside Higher Ed houses a collection of news articles and opinion essays that
put recent developments in online education into long-term context,
including how distance education is affecting learning and the business
models of traditional colleges.

Kennesaw State University (KSU)
Distance Learning Center
1000 Chastain Road, House #58
Kennesaw, GA 30144
(888) 370-2267
Website: http://mooc.kennesaw.edu/courses/k12_online_blended_
learning.php
Kennesaw State University provides K–12 blended and online learning that

takes advantage of its existing technological strengths and infrastructure to offer MOOCs at no cost.

MOOC-Ed Project
Friday Institute for Educational Innovation
1890 Main Campus Drive
Raleigh, NC 27606
(919) 513-8500
Website: http://www.mooc-ed.org
The MOOC-Ed Project provides an overview of current and upcoming MOOCs, the latest research findings from MOOC-Ed courses, and editorials and guest posts focused on education, technology, and course subject matter.

University of Alberta
116 Street and 85 Avenue
Edmonton, AB T6G 2R3
Canada
(780) 492-3111
Website: http://www.ualberta.ca
The University of Alberta plans to be the first Canadian university to offer transfer credits through a MOOC platform.

University of North Carolina at Chapel Hill (UNC)
Campus Box 1020
100 Friday Center Drive
Chapel Hill, NC 27599-1020
(866) 441-3683
Website: http://fridaycenter.unc.edu/moocs

The Friday Center at the University of North Carolina at Chapel Hill serves an ongoing role in the development of noncredit Coursera offerings as well as in the continued expansion of UNC's credit-based online learning opportunities.

University of Toronto
563 Spadina Crescent
Toronto, ON M5S 2J7
Canada
(416) 978-2011
Website: http://www.utoronto.com
The University of Toronto was one of the first Canadian universities to offer MOOCs.

Websites

Because of the changing nature of Internet links, Rosen Publishing has developed an online list of websites related to the subject of this book. This site is updated regularly. Please use this link to access the list:

http://www.rosenlinks.com/DIL/MOOC

FOR FURTHER READING

Bowen, William G. *Higher Education in the Digital Age*. Princeton, NJ: Princeton University Press, 2013.

Hamilton, Diane. *The Online Student's User Manual: Everything You Need to Know to Be a Successful Online College Student*. Lexington, KY: Diane Hamilton, 2010.

Nanfito, Michael. *MOOCs: Opportunities, Impacts, and Challenges: Massive Open Online Courses in Colleges and Universities*. North Charleston, SC: CreateSpace, 2013.

Nixon, Thomas. *Complete Guide to Online High Schools: Distance Learning Options for Teens and Adults*. Fresno, CA: Degree Press, 2012.

O'Shaughnessy, Lynn. *The College Solution: A Guide for Everyone Looking for the Right School at the Right Price*. Upper Saddle River, NJ: FT Press, 2012.

Parker, Robyn E. *Redesigning Courses for Online Delivery: Design, Interaction, Media & Evaluation* (Cutting-Edge Technologies in Higher Education). Bingley, England: Emerald Group Publishing, 2013.

Payton, Theresa M., and Ted Claypoole. *Privacy in the Age of Big Data: Recognizing Threats, Defending Your Rights, and Protecting Your Family*. Lanham, MD: Rowman & Littlefield Publishers, 2014.

Selingo, Jeffrey J. *College Unbound: The Future of Higher Education and What It Means for Students*. Boston, MA: Houghton Mifflin Harcourt, 2013.

Smith, Charles Hugh. *The Nearly Free University and the Emerging Economy: The Revolution in Higher Education*. North Charleston, SC: CreateSpace, 2013.

Voeller, Brad. *Accelerated Distance Learning: The New Way to Earn Your College Degree in the Twenty-First Century*. Spring Branch, TX: Dedicated Publishing, 2011.

BIBLIOGRAPHY

Ackerman, Sherri. "High School Students Try Out for MOOCs." Redefineonline
.org, December 16, 2013. Retrieved March 4, 2014 (http://www
.redefineonline.org/2013/12/high-school-students-try-out-moocs).

Belanger, Yvonne, and J. Thornton. "Bioelectricity: A Quantitative
Approach—Duke University's First MOOC." DukeSpace, 2013.
Retrieved February 8, 2014 (http://dukespace.lib.duke.edu/dspace/
bitstream/handle/10161/6216/Duke_Bioelectricity_MOOC_
Fall2012.pdf?sequence=1).

Blake, David. "MOOCs for the K–12 Set." MOOCs.com, 2013. Retrieved
March 3, 2014 (http://moocs.com/index.php/moocs-for-the
-k-12-set).

Bronson, Perri. "10 Tips About MOOCs." Tivix.com, January 23, 2014.
Retrieved March 4, 2014 (http://www.tivix.com/blog/10-things-
you-should-know-about-moocs).

Campus Explorer. "How to Use MOOCs to Get Your Dream Job." Campus
Explorer. Retrieved February 8, 2014 (http://www.campusexplorer
.com/college-advice-tips/DC5C1E33/How-to-Use-MOOCs
-to-Get-Your-Dream-Job).

Daly, Jimmy. "Credit for MOOCs Is One Step in a Long Journey Toward
Relevance." *EdTech*, September 16, 2013. Retrieved February 8,
2014 (http://www.edtechmagazine.com/higher/article/2013/09/
credit-moocs-one-step-long-journey-toward-relevance).

Green, Emma. "What MOOCs Can't Teach." *Atlantic*, December 2013.
Retrieved March 4, 2014 (http://www.theatlantic.com/events/
archive/2013/12/what-moocs-cant-teach/282402).

Howard, Jennifer. "Publishers See Online Mega-Courses as Opportunity to
Sell Textbooks." *Chronicle of Higher Education*, September 17, 2012.
Retrieved March 3, 2014 (http://chronicle.com/article/Can-MOOCs
-Help-Sell/134446).

McKenna, Laura. "The Big Idea That Can Revolutionize Higher Education: 'MOOC.'" *Atlantic*, May 11, 2012. Retrieved February 3, 2014 (http://www.theatlantic.com/business/archive/2012/05/the-big -idea-that-can-revolutionize-higher-education-mooc/256926).

MOOCs Directory. "Verified Certificate MOOCs." MOOCsUniversity.org. Retrieved March 4, 2014 (http://www.moocs.co/Credits_for_ MOOCS__News.html).

Open Culture, LLC. "MOOQ FAQ." Open Culture. Retrieved March 3, 2014 (http://www.openculture.com/mooc_faq).

Pope, Justin. "What's It Like to Take a MOOC?" *Huffington Post*, August 3, 2013. Retrieved March 4, 2014 (http://www.huffingtonpost.com/ 2013/08/05/what-its-like-mooc_n_3707274.html).

Schmitt, Jeff. "The MOOC Revolution: How to Earn an Elite MBA for Free." *Poets & Quants*, December 17, 2013. Retrieved February 3, 2014 (http://poetsandquants.com/2013/12/17/the-mooc-revolution -how-to-earn-an-elite-mba-for-free).

Shearn, Michael. "Strayer University: An In-Depth Analysis." *Beyond Proxy*, October 17, 2013. Retrieved February 3, 2014 (http://www .beyondproxy.com/strayer-education-analysis).

Voss, Brian D. *Massive Open Online Courses (MOOCs): A Primer for University and College Board Members*. Association of Governing Boards of Universities and Colleges, March 2013. Retrieved March 4, 2014 (http://agb.org/sites/agb.org/files/report_2013_MOOCs pdf).

INDEX

About The Author

Rita Lorraine Hubbard is the author of *Getting a Job in the Food Industry* (Rosen Publishing) and *African Americans of Chattanooga: A History of Unsung Heroes* (The History Press). She is Lee and Low Books' 2012 New Voices Award Winner and is a contributing writer for *Tennessee Women of Vision and Courage*, sponsored by the American Association of University Women. She also manages a writer's blog called *Rita Writes History* and is a media specialist for the *New York Journal of Books*.

Photo Credits

Cover and p. 1 (from left) © iStockphoto.com/muharrem öner, © iStockphoto.com/alexsl, © iStockphoto.com/Warchi, © iStockphoto.com/stocknroll; p. 5 Goodluz/Shutterstock.com; p. 8 Colin MConnell/Toronto Star/Getty Images; p. 9 CarpathianPrince/Shutterstock.com; p. 10 Ryan McVay/Photodisc/Thinkstock; pp. 12, 33 © AP Images; p. 15 The Boston Globe/Getty Images; p. 16 © B Chistopher/Alamy; p. 19 iStockphoto.com/Steve Debenport; p. 22 Klaus Tiedge/iStock/Thinkstock; p. 23 natu/Shutterstock.com; p. 26 Burger/Phanie/SuperStock; p. 36 Comstock/Stockbyte/Thinkstock; p. 38 Andrey_Popov/Shutterstock; cover and interior pages (dots graphic) © iStockphoto.com/suprun; interior pages (browser window graphic) © iStockphoto.com/AF-studio.

Designer: Nicole Russo; Editor: Shalini Saxena